The Agony of Mammon

Also by Lewis H. Lapham

The Agony of Mammon

The Imperial World Economy Explains Itself to the
Membership in Davos, Switzerland

◆

LEWIS H. LAPHAM

VERSO

London · New York

First published by Verso 1998
© Lewis H. Lapham 1998

All rights reserved

VERSO
UK: 6 Meard Street, London W1V 3 HR
US: 180 Varick Street, 10th Floor, New York, NY 10014-4606

VERSO is the imprint of New Left Books

ISBN 1 85984 710 2

British Library Cataloguing in Publication Data
A catalogue record for this book is available from the British Library
Library of Congress Cataloging-in-Publication Data
A catalog record for this book is available from the Library of Congress

Typeset in Garamond by Steven Hiatt, San Francisco
Printed and bound in the USA by R. R. Donnelly & Sons

Contents

For Andrew and Winston

The Agony of Mammon

Poverty is an anomaly to rich people. It is very difficult to make
out why people who want dinner do not ring the bell.
— WALTER BAGEHOT

Although in many ways bountiful and in some ways benign, the colossal mechanism that generates the wealth of nations (a.k.a. "The Global Economy," "Moloch," and "The Invisible Hand") lacks the capacity for human speech or conscious thought, a failing that troubles those of its upper servants who wish to believe that it is they who control the machine and not the machine that controls them. Their *amour propre* forbids them from picturing themselves as mere stokers heaving computer printouts and Montblanc pens (or shopping malls and movie studios and Mexicans) into a blind, remorseless furnace. They seek a more gracious portraiture (as masters of markets, captains of commercial empire), and so, every year in late January, they make their optimistic way from the low-lying places of the earth to the World Economic Forum in Davos, Switzerland, where, high up on the same alp that provided Thomas Mann with the setting for *The Magic Mountain,* they brood upon the mysteries of capitalist creation.

Given the chance last winter to make the annual ascent—the forum's sponsors having waived the $18,984 in various admission and subscription fees in deference to my occupation as an editor and therefore a prospective supplier of supportive adjectives—I didn't see how I could refuse to exercise the option. Here were the people to whom the world's governments assign the task of managing the world's money, and where else could I expect to learn how to divide the price of the deutsche mark by the number of fires in the forests of Brazil, or multiply the number of ships in the Suez Canal by the cost of bombing Iraq?

The advance publicity kindled the glow of great expectation at an altitude of 5,000 feet—five days and six nights of rarefied discussion attended by at least 2,000 gratifyingly important people from 150 countries (heads of state, finance ministers, policy intellectuals, Nobel Prize–winning physicists, corporate executives as thick upon the ground as pine needles), a schedule of continuous briefings on almost any topic that anybody might care to name (the bankruptcy in Djakarta, the future of the Internet, the outlook for Romania), maps of the oil fields around Baku, private viewings of George Soros and Bill Gates.

Traveling from Zurich on the afternoon of Thursday, January 29, I changed trains at Landquart, and during the long and patient climb up the Prättigau, watching the mountains present a succession of picture-postcard views behind shifting foregrounds of noble trees and snowy villages, I passed the time trying to recall something of Mann's novel. I remembered the story ending in the blood-soaked mud of the First World War but the greater part of the narrative taking place at a tuberculosis sanatorium in Davos, and that the moral of the tale addressed the confusions of a ruthlessly acquisitive society lost in the opulent maze of late-nineteenth-century bourgeois capitalism. The principal characters appear as patients afflicted with the symptoms of a disease that Mann associated with the asphyxiations of the spirit induced by too long and too close a confinement in the gilded atmospheres of stupefying wealth. They arrive—an Italian humanist, a Dutch pragmatist, miscellaneous Russian nihilists, et al.—with the several varieties of conventional wisdom then current in Europe, bringing with them the hope of a cure not only for their physical illness but also for their spiritual decay. My memory of the novel was sketchy and incomplete, but I remembered the medical director, the Hofrat Behrens, as a man in a white coat, busy and energetic, brimming with confidence in the apparatus of the scientific method, promising to look in on everybody again tomorrow. I also remembered that nobody got well, and that Mann awarded the part of the anti-hero to a young engineer from Hamburg named Hans Castorp, who doesn't discover, until well after he meets the lovely but disquieting Madame Clavdia

Chauchat, that he's been sent on a fool's errand.

I left the train at Davos-Platz, the next station beyond the one at which Castorp had arrived in the summer of 1907, and although I wasn't met by a tubercular cousin with a yellow carriage and two brown horses, I discovered that I'd been assigned a room at the Berghotel Schatzalp, the once-upon-a-time sanatorium in which Mann had placed his consumptive fugitives from the ballrooms of the Belle Époque. Reached by a funicular railway rising from the town, the building and its glass pavilions had been transformed into a resort hotel in the late 1930s by a Nazi government attentive to the comforts of its senior military officers in need of an occasional respite from the labor of destroying the civilization in which Mann's characters had found nothing worth the trouble to preserve or defend.

While filling out forms at the hotel desk, I asked the concierge whether his guests ever requested any of the rooms once occupied by the characters in Mann's novel. He received the question with a polite but blank smile. Certainly he had heard of the novel (its title and the author's name appeared in the hotel's brochure), but no, none of the guests had ever mentioned it. He didn't go on to say that the hotel catered to a class of people (Italian dress designers, German industrialists, American executives) not likely to take an interest in literary relics, but I judged from his manner, which was brisk and efficient, that questions about the room arrangements in Mann's sanatorium were off the mark, not as far off the mark as questions about the later divisions of space between the Luftwaffe and the Gestapo, but still, now that we were all gathered here on the summit of the new world economic order, not in the best of taste. The assistant manager handed me a key, informed me that the funicular ceased operation at 2 a.m., furnished directions to the ski runs and the spa, and suggested that when at large on the streets of Davos, I would be well-advised to walk around in rubber-soled boots.

"For the ice," he said, "especially at night, when the ice is not always easy to see."

It was nearly dark by the time I'd admired the majestic views from each of the hotel's several points of vantage and descended again to the long and winding promenade that serves as Davos's principal thoroughfare. Not finding a shop that sold rubber-soled boots, I walked with some care to the Congress Centre, which had been reconstructed in 1990 for the express purpose of accommodating the World Economic Forum's annual meeting. Fitted to the bleak forms of the modern institutional style and much of its sizeable bulk concealed behind and below a steep escarpment, the Congress Centre presented a very low profile to the public street, the impression of a heavily fortified artillery emplacement strengthened by the presence of Swiss soldiers armed with machine guns.

The passing of the security clearance took as much time as the similar procedures at the White House, and once through the last of the checkpoints, I found myself caught up in a loud commotion of noise and light. Meetings had been in progress since early that morning, and my first impression was that of the United Nations building in New York during an outbreak of bad news in West Africa—a great many self-absorbed people hurrying to and fro with documents of immense significance, a welter of languages (predominantly English but also a good deal of French and German), television crews filming stand-ups of Elie Wiesel and the president of Argentina, nearly everybody talking on cellular phones. The pretty girl at the registration desk handed me a white badge marked with my name and passport photograph as well as a computer code granting access to the forum's interior lines of communication. To be worn around the neck at all times, the badge identified me as a participant, and therefore a person of consequence accorded a higher rank than the members of the working press, who received orange badges and were to be looked upon with the correct balance of pity and contempt. Another pretty girl behind a different desk presented me with a canvas shoulder bag stuffed with a sheaf of printed instructions—a plan of the Congress Centre, a directory listing the names and titles of all the other participants (well over a thousand pages of small print), elusive references to last year's meeting (unanimous in its failure to foresee the Asian economic collapse), a guide to the better restaurants in town.

But even with the instructions firmly in hand, I was still at a loss to know which of the late-afternoon briefings to attend, the one about El Niño or the one about robots. Unable to resolve the dilemma and while waiting for Helmut Kohl, the chancellor of Germany, to deliver the forum's opening address, I found a table in one of the Congress Centre's five cafés and read through the homework assignment in the canvas bag. The forum had chosen "Priorities for the 21st Century" as its theme for 1998, and the printed materials glistened with four-color advertisements announcing the presence in Davos of an impressive number of the world's leading corporations (among them DuPont, Volkswagen, Swissair, Texaco and Anderson Consulting) dressed up in full philanthropic regalia and setting about the work of "broadening horizons" and "finding harmony in diversity." A program of events listed the place, time, and principal speakers for each of the 310 sessions scheduled over the term of the forum in the Congress Centre's twelve halls and conference rooms as well as in one or another of twenty-seven resort hotels, and I was surprised to see that the expected briefings on political and economic topics were interspersed with a good many discussions of a more metaphysical nature—the implications of the human genome project, the problem of death and dying, the meaning of clones. The names on the program suggested a division of the prominent people on the set into three classifications—as many as 1,000 business executives representing corporate assets of roughly $4 trillion (i.e., a sum exceeding the collective net worth of all the member governments of the United Nations); 500 politicians; and 500 intellectuals in various denominations, a few of them famous, most of them futurists.

Before I could read through the whole of the book, and just as I turned the page to session seventy-one ("China Business Networking"), I noticed that the badge around the neck of the man seated across the table identified him as a traveler from Beijing. Thinking to begin a conversation and pointing to the page in the book, I said something to the effect that in China these days business presumably was booming.

"Oh yes," he said. "Four years ago, zero cellular telephones; now, twenty million cellular telephones. Four years ago, no pagers; now, forty million pagers."

Smiling with the zeal of an enthusiast converted to a new religion, he looked to be about twenty-seven years old, certain of his facts and undoubtedly possessed of enough statistics to justify the building of a fertilizer plant in Harbin, a nuclear weapons factory in Xinjiang, or a golf course in Shanghai. We managed to talk only briefly because he was late for a meeting with some people from Motorola, but in those few minutes I heard the first faint statement of what I would come to know as the forum's dominant leitmotif. The man from Beijing didn't intend any such statement, musical or otherwise; he made it inadvertently, by way of an offhand remark while excusing himself to keep his appointment on Promenade Entry Level 3.

"You know," he said, "in China we're spending $750 billion for infrastructures, but in the last two months we laid off one million railroad workers. You could say that our lack of democracy is a blessing. In Europe or America there would be arguments."

Kohl arrived late and spoke in German. His presence attracted a standing-room-only crowd to the Congress Hall, the largest of the forum's auditoria, and among the well-dressed heads in the audience

I recognized several American newspaper columnists as well as a number of corporation presidents whose photographs I had seen in the pages of *Fortune* and *Business Week*. Cameras placed at different angles in the hall projected the chancellor's image onto a large television screen behind the podium, the magnification exaggerating Kohl's resemblance to a gigantic bird of prey gazing mournfully down on a row of field mice. He had come to say that the Economic and Monetary Union was an accomplished fact about which he didn't wish to hear any further complaint. Yes, it was going to be difficult—everything was always difficult—but what was done was done. The votes had been counted by the authorities in Brussels, the presses in Frankfurt were busy printing the new euro currency that would begin circulating on January 1, 2002, and Kohl was sick of listening to all the pointless talk about possible social and political consequences. His irritation prompted him to regret that the pessimists in London and Copenhagen never had the chance to know his mother, a marvelous woman, as wise as she was strong-minded, who taught her children to eat the meals placed in front of them on the kitchen table without sniveling objection. "We learned to clean up our plates," he said. Germany had cleaned up its plate (i.e., accepted the financial discipline required by the Maastricht Treaty), and now it was time for the Italians, and for everybody else in Europe, to clean up their plates. The euro was good for people, and the sooner they learned to like it the better.

Kohl spoke at ponderous length, and I noticed that we were free to wander out into the lobby for a phone call or an exchange of business cards before returning to our seats to listen to the chancellor's extended remarks. During one of my own brief absences, I ran across Peter Foges, a producer of television documentaries for PBS whom I knew in New York as a close student of both the stock market and German romanticism. He informed me that because I was a participant (white badge, not orange), I belonged to what the forum's sponsors denominated as the "Club of Media Leaders." The honorific brought with it an invitation to dinner later that evening at the Hotel Rinaldi, a dinner that Foges encouraged me to attend. He had been coming to the annual meeting in Davos for five years, most recently in his capacity as the producer of *Adam Smith's Money World,* and he recognized me as a novice in need of additional program notes.

The restaurant at the Hotel Rinaldi looked like a tourist postcard—beamed ceilings, beer steins behind the bar, decorative wood carvings, the waitresses dressed as if for a village scene in *The Sound of Music*—and most of the other media leaders in the room were American journalists with whom I was acquainted under their less exalted titles as staff writers for *The New Yorker,* contributors to *Newsweek* and *The Wall Street Journal,* the editor of *Foreign Affairs.* An august company, but one that I never had seen in such low spirits. The Monica Lewinsky story was only two weeks old, and it had done a good deal of damage to everybody's self-esteem. President Clinton had let them down—mortified them in front of their European peers, reduced their news organizations to the rank of grocery-store tabloids, called into question their own reputations as custodians of the American conscience, protectors of the public morals. How could the man behave so badly? Yes, they had known that Clinton was an inveterate philanderer and reckless with the truth—had known as much before he was first elected to the presidency in the autumn of 1992—but with a White House intern? A fat girl? From California and apparently hatched from the script of one of Aaron Spelling's evening soap operas? It was intolerable. Beyond all reason. Not to be endured.

The displays of wounded dignity took up the whole of the cocktail hour, and then at dinner the conversation turned to Saddam Hussein, the progenitor of the other outrage visible that week on the front pages of the world's newspapers. Interpreted as variations on the theme of humiliation and defeat, the two stories served as a joint indictment of the United States as a flatulent hegemon, isolationist and smug, weakened by a president who couldn't keep his fingers out of pies. Hussein was clearly a monster, a madman who must be suppressed, but where would the Americans find the necessary moral authority?

Both the tenor and substance of the talk suggested that the American media leaders wished to be perceived as statesmen come to Davos to talk about matters of serious concern—about the devaluation of Thailand's baht, the collapse of the Indonesian rupiah and the Korean won, about the likely effect of the Asian economic crisis in Tokyo and Moscow, about why the United States Congress (a sad collection of provincial politicians, many of them barely literate, nearly all of them badly dressed) refused to ratify the fast-track trade legislation, blocked the appropriations for the International Monetary Fund, and declined to pay the $1.5 billion owed by the United States to the UN. The global economy apparently had replaced the Cold War as the heavy subject about which one was expected to be deeply informed if one was to retain one's standing as a journalist of rank. The old "domino theory" had been supplanted by the theory of "contagion," which referred to the spreading of fiscal and monetary disease from one country to the next. Whereas once it had been understood that unless communism could be contained in the jungles of Vietnam the virus would show up on the beaches of Southern California, now it was understood that large-scale bankruptcy in almost any of the world's markets (regional, emerging, peripheral) was likely to infect the prices on the New York Stock Exchange. Care must be taken, "crony capitalists" brought to book, irresponsible currency speculators made to swallow the pills of "austerity." The after-dinner speaker, an economics professor from MIT named Rudi Dornbusch, set forth the preferred attitude toward the financial ruin in the Indonesian archipelago.

"It's important that some people lose a lot of money," Dornbusch said. "Important that they be punished for their stupidity and greed."

His phrase "some people" embraced not only the friends and family of President Suharto but also the Japanese and European banks that had placed fanciful loans all over the roulette table of southern Asia, to no purpose other than their own selfish and myopic gain. The American journalists in the room received the professor's remarks with a show of complacent nods, glad of the chance to recover some of the pride they had lost to their foreign counterparts during the discussion of Saddam's intransigence and Monica's beret. Because American investors had underwritten a smaller share of the Asian risk, which was beginning to look as if it might cost the European banks upwards of $20 billion, the ladies and gentlemen from New York and Washington had found solace, at least for the moment, in a thinly smiling air of superiority.

They also took pleasure in the humiliation of Japan. Five or six years ago the Japanese economy was being touted as the wonder of the world; Japanese banks were buying California, Japanese businessmen were touring the Washington lecture circuit with little sermons about the spendthrift Americans who had lost their knack for making cars. But now that the Tokyo real-estate market had fallen upon stony ground, the shoe was on the other foot, and it was possible to speak of the once sovereign shogunate of the Pacific Rim as a nation famous for the incidence of suicide among the officials in its finance ministry.

Together with the gossip current in the corridors of the Congress Centre, the journalists at dinner offered suggestions about which briefings to attend, how to get invited to the Coca-Cola reception, where to find the Bolivians, when to order the raclette. The evening ended with the company ordering a last bottle of white wine, with Dornbusch deploring what he called "Dial 1-800-BAILOUT for reckless businessmen, greedy bankers, and corrupt politicians," and with a melancholy reprise on the theme of big Bill Clinton's penis.

Walking with Foges along the promenade in the direction of the Berghotel's funicular, still looking out for the invisible ice and thinking again of the cases of advanced or terminal narcissism among the characters in Mann's novel, I remarked on the odds against bringing the World Economic Forum's purpose into intelligible focus.

"If you think that you're missing the point," Foges said, "don't worry about it. Everybody misses the point. Something more important is always happening somewhere else."

By the end of the day on Friday I'd become sufficiently familiar with the forum's procedures to know that I was always going to be in the wrong place at the wrong time—that if I was in the Flüela restaurant listening to a functionary from the International Monetary Fund discuss the outlook for Thailand, then I should have been at the Waldhaus Grill, listening to four Bulgarians talk about trucks. But I'd attended enough briefings to begin to form a set of coherent impressions, and I'd come to understand the limitations of the white badge, which granted access not only to the forum's numerous meeting rooms but also, without first having to arrange an appointment, to any of the other participants. The privilege was helpful but not without its difficulties. The print on the badges was too small to read at the decisive distance of four feet, and because protocol forbade too crass a weighing up of a fellow participant's prospective worth, random encounters in a coffee bar or hotel lobby proceeded along the lines of an Easter egg hunt. One was obliged to open the conversation without knowing the significance of the person to whom one was already in the midst of making a pleasant remark about the chance of snow or terrorism. It was possible to discover the Australian finance minister or the chief executive officer of Dassault Aviation; it was also possible to blunder into another media leader almost as poorly informed as oneself.

None of the participants lacked for lists of impressive statistics—250 million children in the world working for a few cents an hour; 50 percent of the world's population without electricity, 70 percent without telephones, Japanese banks burdened with bad debt in the amount of $550 billion—and second only to "contagion," the most solemn word in any conversation was "transparency," by which was meant full disclosure of another country's politics, another company's marketing plan, somebody else's money. Just as contagion was always bad, transparency was always good (like "dialogue" and "reduced labor costs"), and what had gone wrong in Asia (in Korea as well as in Indonesia and Thailand) was the general failure to produce enough transparency.

Nor was it difficult to take the point that although each and every one of the forum's 2,000 participants was important, some were more important than others. The conversations apt to lead to a specific result (the building of a dam in Chile, say, or the writing of the Multilateral Agreement on Investments) took place privately, the time and place and principal speakers omitted from the program. The morning and afternoon discussions in the Congress Centre served the same purpose as the golf and tennis games arranged for the guests attending a conference at the Aspen Institute—a chance to acquire contacts, enlarge spheres of access, possibly drum up an invitation to dinner with the president of Mexico.

The division of interest that remained as constant as the weather—bright blue sky, the temperature at thirty degrees, no wind, very little ice—was the distinction between the buyers and the sellers. The buyers (bankers and industrialists from the wealthy nations) worried about transparency; the sellers (politicians and government ministers from the poorer countries) worried about paying their hotel bills. The buyers delighted in grand abstractions and the illusions of omnipotence. Like the characters in Mann's *Magic Mountain,* they were accustomed to the deference of wine stewards, and although they couldn't draw upon the novelist's acquaintance with the music of Richard Wagner and the writing of Friedrich Nietzsche they were heirs to the dream of the *übermensch,* and they had brought with them in their hand-sewn luggage what the correspondent for London's *Financial Times* estimated at "roughly 70% of the world's daily output of self-congratulation."

The sellers hustled investment opportunities, and all their numbers were as bright and shiny as the exhibits at a trade show—low inflation, high growth, willing workers, beautiful girls, democratic institutions springing up like mushrooms, responsible fiscal policies, broad vistas, a compliant press, courageous police. Their will to please spoke to the terms and conditions of post-modern imperialism—the lesser nations of the earth become colonies not of governments but of corporations, the law of nations construed as the rule of money, and the world's parliaments intimidated by the force of capital in much the same way that in the eighteenth and nineteenth centuries they had been intimidated by the force of arms. Once upon a time, and even as recently as forty years ago, the community of business interests tended to look upon the politicians as representatives of a superior power; merchants took the trouble to learn the languages south and east of Suez, to send sympathetic agents and maybe presents, seeking an audience with the empress or the king. No longer. Not under the dispensation of a global marketplace conducted in English and held together by McDonald's golden arches and the news on CNN. Now the kings and empresses kiss the ring of commerce.

An exceptionally blunt demonstration of the revised imperialist thesis took place in one of the Congress Centre's smaller meeting rooms before a discriminating audience of American oil-company presidents and French suppliers of municipal infrastructure. A Belgian business executive in a well-cut suit sat on a small stage with three Russian bureaucrats, all of whom looked as if they recently had escaped from one of Chekhov's provincial town meetings, and after introducing each of them in turn, he smiled upon his fellow participants as if he had brought them gifts of rare and precious fur.

"Here we have three active, successful, real-life politicians," he said. "They wish to make important statements."

The Russians spoke in succession from stage left to stage right, like accordion players performing a set of variations on *Moscow Nights*. Some of the translation was hard to follow, but not the principal points of interest: yes, it was true, Russia was a difficult business environment ("still some chaos"), but Russian enterprises had begun to pay salaries ("we have real government, real president, two chambers of parliament"); Russian exports weren't being dumped on international markets ("we wouldn't do that to our good friends, the Europeans"); crime was receding ("here in Russia we have learned how to get the criminals into the investment process"); foreign investors didn't pay taxes until their deals returned a profit ("remember America in the nineteenth century, wonderful place, no antitrust laws"); and 18,000 feet of pipe had been drilled into the Caspian basin without yet hitting bottom in what appeared to be an ocean of oil.

At the end of their recitation the Russians fell abruptly silent, their faces as stolid as cement, their hands clasped patiently on their knees, their innocent blue eyes staring innocently off into the innocent blue distance of the Siberian steppe. The Belgian sponsor was immediately on his feet, talking rapidly into the nearest microphone: "What we have heard, gentlemen," he said, "is exciting news. Stability in Moscow, flexibility in the regions, higher confidence for 'ninety-eight. A bumpy road, *meine Herren*, but in the end, great riches."

The buyers weren't so sure. What they had heard about Russia inclined them to think that foreign money had as much chance of surviving a Russian winter as did the armies of Hitler and Napoleon. Seventy-nine bankers had been shot to death in Moscow or St. Petersburg over the course of the last four years, and some of the other Russians in Davos—not the bureaucrats but the ones who arrived by helicopter with flashy blonde women and suitcases of American currency—didn't seem to have acquired, at least not quite yet, a proper sense of capitalist decorum. They preferred vodka to mineral water, they didn't attend the sessions about the prudent management of long-term corporate growth, and their female companions didn't sign up for horse-drawn sleigh excursions to the picturesque village of Clavadel.

Small windrows of doubt drifted across the foreheads of the executives gathering their notes and making ready to depart for the next round of briefings. An oil-company president said that in Russia the criminals were easier to deal with than the politicians ("At least they stay bought"). Somebody else said, "Can you imagine meeting those three guys on a road twenty miles west of Sverdlovsk? They'd make a joke of forcing you to choose between giving them your wife or your car." The editor of a financial newsletter explained that it was no easy trick getting the oil safely away from the Caspian basin. No long-distance pipelines had been put in place, and the possible routes (via the Caucasus to the Black Sea or the Mediterranean, from Kazakhstan to China, through Iran to Kharg Island, via Pakistan and Afghanistan to India and the Arabian Sea, through Russia to Ukraine) were all, in the editor's word, "problematic." "We're talking about bandits," he said. "About people draining oil out of a pipeline in the same way they would take milk from a goat."

Talk about bandits occupied the conversation that same evening at dinner, again at the Hotel Rinaldi, when Bill Richardson, the US ambassador to the United Nations, briefed the club of media leaders on the topic of Saddam Hussein. Speaking to a larger crowd than had listened to the *dicta* of Rudi Dornbusch, Richardson cast his remarks in a tone of voice that was both flatteringly elusive (a statesman in the company of fellow-statesmen) and frankly exasperated (the plain-spoken American, open-hearted and gregarious, confronted with the moral equivalent of pond scum). The Security Council that week was preparing to vote on an American resolution to bomb Baghdad if Iraq didn't satisfy the demands of the UN weapons inspectors, and Richardson was traveling the world in search of support for the recommended course of punishment. Madeline Albright, the secretary of state, was talking to Britain and France; Richardson was canvassing the less prominent members of the Security Council. That morning he had been in Sweden, but he had stopped off in Davos (on his way to Gabon and Brazil) because he didn't want to lose the chance of clarifying the American position ("off the record, of course, and not for attribution") before so distinguished a caucus of the world's most important journalists.

Presenting the United States as a victim of circumstance, not at all the kind of country that went around looking for cities to bomb, Richardson began with a series of rhetorical questions. What else could one do? Where and how was one supposed to draw the line, either on a map or in the sand? Hussein didn't listen to reason, didn't keep his word, wasn't about to quit manufacturing weapons of mass destruction.

"God damn it," he said, "the man wants to be bombed."

The assertion didn't prompt anybody in the room to second the motion, and a British correspondent put the palpable skepticism in the form of a question.

"Then why do him the favor?"

"Nobody's doing anybody any favors," Richardson said. "We're preserving America's credibility, not allowing the UN to be so contemptuously insulted."

Another correspondent asked Richardson how he presented his argument to the governments from whom he sought endorsement, governments possibly worried about the effect on Arab opinion, or the chance that Hussein might respond by sending an anthrax-bearing missile into downtown Tel Aviv.

"It's not an easy sell," Richardson said. "First I take our best diplomatic shot. I say that Hussein is Hitler, that the diplomatic options have been exhausted, that we don't mean to obliterate Iraq but merely to bring it into full compliance. Then I move in with the killer argument—look, I say, if you don't support us, get out of the way because we will send the bombers no matter what you decide to do."

Still in the character of the exasperated man, the man "sick of using words like 'serious consequences'" and then seeing those words ignored as if they were nothing more than cheap cigar smoke, Richardson agreed to answer any further questions that anybody cared to ask. All the journalists in the room accepted the ambassador's disclaimer about his remarks being "off the record" as an invitation to convey them loudly to Saddam, and the impromptu press conference wandered off into the land of the surreal:

Q. "How much bombing?"

A. "We have three kinds of bombing—pinprick, substantial, and massive. Pinprick won't do. We would want the bombing to be substantial."

Q. "And the reaction from other Arab states?"

A. "We'll take a big hit in the Arab world. But we can live with that."

Q. "And what if Iraq strikes Israel with nerve gas?"

A. "We've thought about that, too. There may be some spillage."

Q. "What if China vetoes the resolution in the Security Council?"

A. "We'll go ahead and bomb anyway. China wants to be a great power, but doesn't know how."

Several correspondents asked questions about what the United States meant to do after the bombs had come and gone. What was the next move, "the end game," and how would America know that its purposes had been achieved? Richardson wasn't sure; substantial damage, certainly, which would show up on the satellite photographs, and maybe some sort of popular uprising on the part of the Iraqi people, a revolution about which the ambassador was at liberty to say nothing except that the United States had "wonderful information" from sources inside Iraq, information that had cost the US

$35 billion, and "at those rates it better be good." At the end of little more than an hour the questioning subsided into listless re-phrasings and repetitions, and Richardson, still on message, still bristling with threats, hurried off to tell his fierce story to other voices in other rooms.

Worries about security—security for private investment, security for regional capital markets and corporate communications systems, security for public institutions, for civil society, for Western civili-zation—bulked large in the conversation at Davos, and the same questions kept coming up in different contexts, different languages, different conference rooms. Not surprisingly, given the ample wealth and assured status of the participants, most of the worry was about the future. For the time being, the good old invisible hand could be relied upon to distribute very handsome stock options, quite a few of them in denominations of $10 million and $20 million, but how long would the good fortune last, and if it wasn't going to last, where on the horizon could one expect to see the heralds of doom? Speaking in which language and bringing what blood-soaked remnant of whose severed head?

Not that anybody doubted the sacred truths of *laissez-faire* capi-talism or questioned the sublime wisdom of the bottom line. All present understood that the free market was another name for God, but then again, when one got to thinking about it, the market, like God, didn't always answer everybody's prayers, and some of the more anxious members of the troupe had begun to wonder whether they remained (as the public-relations officers assured them they did) the masters of their fate and the captains of their destiny.

The abruptness of last year's financial collapse in Asia had come as something of a nasty surprise, and maybe the world was a more uncertain place than one might guess sitting here on the terrace of the Berghotel Schatzalp, admiring the plum cake and enjoying the view of the Rinerhorn. Just read the newspapers or listen to one of those policy-institute intellectuals at the Congress Centre talk about Rwanda or the Balkans, or about the Russians raffling off their inventories of nuclear weapons, or that awful story in the *International Herald Tribune,* the one about the Italian businessman kidnapped eight months ago in Brescia. The family had been slow with the ransom money, and the kidnappers were sending little pieces of the businessman's ears (last month the left ear, yesterday the right), as reminders of the outstanding debt.

No sir, it wasn't always easy to justify the market's ways to man. Not that anybody knew how else to proceed, but the market was damned hard to figure, and sometimes it could be downright mean. Which was the reason for all the walking around with the badges and the briefing books—to see if it might be possible to come up with a means of teaching the market how to behave in a civilized manner, maybe tempering its cruelty (which wasn't the market's fault, but merely a fact of its nature) with at least the facsimile of a conscience. A large project and a complex task, and not one to be addressed lightly, but if the men at Davos didn't undertake it, who else would? Who else could sow the wilderness of the free market with the seeds of moral scruple?

At session number fifty-three, "International Corruption: How Can Companies Play by the Rules and Still Win?" the participants assembled in the Salève Room reviewed the lessons of bitter experience. Seated in round, cream-colored leather chairs, they began by exchanging cautionary tales—about the legendary rapacity of Nigerian oil and finance ministers, about the different methods of laundering money in warm and cold climates, about the competitive advantage enjoyed by German manufacturers, who could write off their annual payments of $2 billion in bribes as a tax-deductible expense. The several narratives prompted a number of general observations. Corruption was more prevalent in those countries that insisted on stringent forms of government regulation because no poorly paid public servant in one of the dustier places of the earth could refuse a gratuity of $50,000 from a handsome CEO wearing Italian shoes and a British suit. The poor man would find it hard to look the CEO straight in the eyes, probably would think that he was looking into the face of Quetzalcóatl.

Even so, systematic bribery was preferable, at least in the short term, to random bribery, because "then it becomes a rational cost." But in the long term, bribery under any of its aliases was the enemy of global freedom and bad for economic growth. Bridges and dams collapsed because the money allocated for steel beams financed the prime minister's harem or the general's zoo, and people died in large numbers, which didn't improve local attitudes toward international business corporations. The habit of paying bribes also corrupted the people on the high side of the money. Let the fine gentlemen from London or Dusseldorf become overly adept at dealing dishonestly with others, and sooner or later they learned to become dishonest with themselves, and their own annual reports began to read as if they had been composed under a ceiling fan in Abuja.

Nor was it easy to know how to go about being both a good Christian and a successful capitalist, how to join the act of pitiless self-seeking with the gesture of turning the other cheek, how to balance the observation that what is moral usually doesn't pay against the belief that what pays is, by definition, moral. The delegate from Kenya expressed the dilemma in a remark about borrowing money from the World Bank, which required its loan applicants to first sign a protocol promising not to engage in corrupt practices. It was a handsome and uplifting thought, but standard African business practice being somewhat less than perfect, how then did one buy the tractors, the medicine, or the wheat? The international lending agencies also obliged their clients to protect the borrowed money with high interest rates, which preserved the integrity of the balance sheet but wrecked the hope of economic growth. On the other hand, if the borrowing country offered its citizens the privilege of cheap credit, the foreign banks took away the loans.

Further concerns about the barbarism of the free market emerged in a conversation over lunch at the Seehof Hotel in a sequence of questions and answers arranged around the topic of corporate espionage. Once again the participants came up against the problem of "transparency" and the need for people to tell one another the truth, not only about their bank credit but also about their friends and associates in the drug trade. Some of the civilized countries could rely on clean and well-lighted regulatory agencies, but as the world's markets became increasingly competitive, the prudent businessman was well-advised to take precautions. Every technique known to government intelligence services during the long, dark night of the Cold War (electronic surveillance, blackmail, disinformation, telephone intercepts, timely traffic accidents) had been privatized by unscrupulous corporations eager to steal their competitors' customer lists and product designs. Any company of sufficient size should assume that in somebody's mind it was "a fat target," its computer system probably invaded, its proprietary information almost certainly being sold, at prices running to six and seven figures, by executives recently downsized. The kidnapping of corporate executives meanwhile was fast becoming a growth industry, not only in Italy and Mexico but also in Belgium and the United States, and the kingdom of organized crime was beginning to resemble the Holy Roman Empire. Conceive of its several thrones and dominions as subsidiaries of a single global conglomerate, and the sum of its collective enterprise would exceed the GDP reported by most of the world's economies.

If the several concerns about security formed the highest-priority discussion in Davos, the next most urgent subject of general conversation was the euro—guesses as to how and why it would transform European society, speculation about its likely effect on the American dollar, theories about its political origin and historical meaning. The argument in favor of the new currency presented it as a *deus ex machina* guaranteed to make the collective European economy more competitive in the world's markets, and its promoters projected an immense upwelling of surplus energy: more jobs, greater profits, braver hopes, a vigorous rising from what were said to be the velvet sofas of the welfare state. The terms of the Maastricht Treaty obliged the signatories to reduce government expenditures for the comforts of everyday life (free education and health care, generous unemployment benefits, no end of music festivals, etc.), which was a decision none too soon in coming because the European corporate sector could no longer afford to pay the carrying costs. Not if the manufacturers of private wealth wished to keep pace with the Asians and the Americans.

The changes, of course, wouldn't take hold at once, and during the brief period of delay, while the benevolence of the public sector was being transferred to the no doubt equally benevolent offices of the private sector, a certain number of people might experience "disruptions" and "dislocations," possibly even a few moments of temporary "discomfort" and short bouts of "austerity." The inconvenience couldn't be helped, and it certainly wasn't anything to worry about—more like the few minutes of turbulence encountered on a weekend flight from London to Biarritz than like a bread riot in Weimar Germany.

The apostles of the new economic order were ripe with cautionary tales, and it wasn't much trouble to find a banker at one of the conference's café tables eager to talk about confiscatory tax rates and government bureaucracy suffocating the genius of invention—Germany cosseting its workers with six weeks of vacation and another twenty-seven days of sick leave, 3,000 young Frenchmen leaving Paris every month because no employer could afford to hire them (not at what amounted to $140 an hour when one added the cost of the mandatory emoluments), unemployed workers in Lyon swollen with the gall to demand paid vacations from their paid idleness, the once industrious citizens of Hamburg become as lazy as Italians, as indolent as Greeks, refusing to condescend to menial labor because they enjoyed a higher standard of luxury when living on the dole. Some respondents spoke of leeches; others mentioned parasites or the rock of Sisyphus, but all agreed that the burdens were insupportable, the feckless charity synonymous with ruin. Look what happened to Russia, and know that socialism by any other name is still stupidity or disease; look at China and know that the keys of capitalist free enterprise can unlock even the most abominable of Marxist dungeons. The promoters of the euro never tired of citing the Chinese example, and they were especially fond of Li Lanquing, the vice premier of the People's Republic, who appeared one morning on the great stage of the Congress Hall to deliver what was regarded as an inspiring speech.

Sympathetic to the concerns of his capitalist friends confronted with the prospects of a little deprivation, Mr. Li began by observing that China was no stranger to the "challenges" of "economic restructuring and enterprise reform." In China, 87,000 state enterprises were on their way to being privatized, which in turn meant that 112 million workers probably would be scrapped. Not an easy or pleasant task, said Mr. Li, but one that must be squarely faced. For how else do countries find their way into the garden of prosperity if not by crossing the river of austerity?

"On the one bank of the river," he said, "we have the traditional planned economy; on the other, the socialist market economy. Now, most Chinese enterprises have crossed the river and are doing well after adapting themselves to the environment and law of the market economy. ... But some other enterprises are still struggling to cross the river by various means: some by swimming, others by boat, and still others by building bridges. I believe that in three years' time, most of them will get on shore successfully. However, since this is a river crossing, some may be drowned."

The audience in the Congress Hall welcomed Mr. Li's parable with grateful applause. A village tale, so simply and inspiringly told. Drowning in the Weser or the Marne was perhaps not as instructive as being washed away in the floodwaters of the Yangtze, but the lesson was the same and well worth bearing in mind when the bus drivers in Mainz or Lille began to complain about the loss of their paid vacation days.

Because the meeting in Davos represented a quorum of investors rather than an assembly of citizens, and because the advantages implicit in the euro clearly would accrue to the accounts of large businesses and the central banks, it was no surprise that sentiment in its favor heavily outweighed the expressions of suspicion or mistrust. Of the skeptics I encountered in the Congress Centre or the town, the majority seemed to be French, and none more inclined to argument than the provincial mayor whom I first mistook for a Parisian intellectual late Friday evening in the bar at the National Hotel. A handsome man in his early fifties, modishly dressed in a turtleneck sweater and a tweed suit, he made no secret of his joy in words, and to a lovely young lady who admired his watch but missed his references to Robespierre and Talleyrand, he was explaining the Maastricht Treaty as an economic means to a political end, a government by fiat, a new social contract drafted by accountants and administered by a bank in Frankfurt. Wonderful in theory, he said, but maybe not so wonderful in fact. Suppose the common coinage of the euro didn't result in the happy circumstances envisioned by Louis Vuitton and Chancellor Kohl? Suppose the good news was a little slow in coming? What then? He shrugged his shoulders and said that he could see, alas all too easily, barricades in the Rue St. Honoré, and the tumbrels rolling across the cobblestones of the Place Vendôme.

The young lady associated the Rue St. Honoré with the Hotel Bristol and Dior, and she wasn't much interested in tumbrels. She drifted away to more up-tempo company at the other end of the bar, and her abrupt departure prompted her abandoned tutor to an amused smile.

"Never will you see a more elegant proof of the great theorem of globalization," he said. "Like ducks or hummingbirds, they come to Davos from as far away as Iceland and the Canary Islands."

Inviting me to join him in a final glass of calvados, he introduced himself as the mayor of a town in Acquitaine, an exporter of wine and an historian manqué with a particular interest in the Napoleonic Wars. In his capacity as both citizen and politician, he favored the idea of government in the hands of enlightened public servants, people educated at the écoles supèrieures who could be counted upon to care for French history as well as for the gardens and the trees. The provenience of the euro he traced to the fear of German militarism. At the end of the Second World War it was thought that if the Germans could be brought peaceably into the concert of Europe, maybe they wouldn't need the reassurance of a new Bismarck or another Hitler. A pleasant thought and a hopeful proposition, but not unless Europe was governed by people as civilized as the French. Which, sadly, wasn't the way things had worked out. The Economic and Monetary Union assigned the power of decision to the mechanism of "the free market," which didn't know how to read and write, much less think. Nothing good could come from so crude a form of Anglo-Saxon idolatry. The privatization of the state monopolies undoubtedly would enrich the business interests taking title to the assets, possibly would gratify the vanity of the financiers keen to overthrow the sovereignty of the American dollar, certainly would reduce the cost of transporting eels from San Sebastian to Stockholm and Salerno. But would the coming of the euro lower commodity prices and the unemployment rate, discover a constitution in a balance sheet, make politics out of Belgian chocolate? The mayor didn't think so.

"A credible currency," he said, "depends upon credible government, and who are the people who will tell the Italians that they
must sing and dance like Dutchmen? A country that gives up
control of its own money lets go the reins of its destiny, and when
events get out of hand in Portugal or Finland, what kind of help do
you think will be arriving from the bank managers in Frankfurt?"

The question answered itself, and the mayor, pleased with his
rhetorical flourishes, began a disquisition on the difference between
the French and British attitudes toward oysters, the one statist and
therefore benevolent, the other subject to market forces and therefore swinish. Time didn't permit my listening to the whole of the
speech, not if I hoped to reach the Berghotel Schatzalp on the
funicular. Promising the mayor that tomorrow I would remind him
of the place at which he'd left off his argument, I found my way
back to the promenade and thence, together with two gentlemen in
black overcoats, neither of them wearing identification badges or in
a mood to speak English, up through the pine trees to the once-
upon-a-time sanatorium where Ludovico Settembrini taught the
young Hans Castorp to appreciate the virtues of philistinism and
the beauty of bourgeois piano music.

Early the next morning at a breakfast table on the hotel terrace, high
up in the light of a new day beginning its descent into the doll-like
town of Davos, I made a list of the questions that I meant to ask Dr.
Klaus Schwab, the World Economic Forum's founder, chief apolo-
gist, guidance counselor and spiritual director. We had arranged an

interview for 10 o'clock, and although I didn't anticipate much of a
resemblance to the Hofrat Behrens (no white coat, no stethoscope, a
Swiss academic in place of the German clinician), I had been told, by
Foges and a correspondent for one of the London papers, that Professor Schwab tended to classify the several forms of economic malady
under the rubrics of physical illness, speaking of capital markets
that were "feverish" or "consumptive," of a "palsied" GDP or a
"suppurating" trade balance. It was also said of the professor that he
appreciated careful preparation, and so, well-supplied with coffee
and sweet rolls, I set about the chore of reading through what had
become an extensive collection of scattered notes—informal asides
entered in the margins of formal briefing documents (about "cross-
cultural moral judgments" and "the outlook for Kazakhstan"), lists
of possibly significant statistics (Japan's economy eight times larger
than China's; 85 percent of the world's capital held by private investors; Korean Air Lines offered for sale at a price less than that of a
single Boeing 747); fragments of conversations overheard in the
corridors of the Congress Centre ("I'm a pacifist, but if we're going
to have a war, we might as well win it"), descriptive phrases, remarks unavailable to attribution or direct quotation. Many of the
notes were no longer valid, an impression acquired on Thursday
having been corrected by a fact turned up on Friday, but a surprising
number of them recalled a still memorable scene or tone of
voice—Elie Wiesel, very much in the character of moralist-in-resi-
dence, parsing the text of the Davos meeting for a young woman
from Mexican television ("Nowhere else will you find a conference

at which so many captains of industry are speaking about the soul");
Archbishop Desmond Tutu, surrounded by a cadre of zealous admir-
ers in the Photo Café, loudly demanding to know what the European central banks meant to do about rescuing the price of South
African gold; Shoichiro Toyoda, the chairman of Toyota, defending
the honor of Japanese business with an arrangement of clichés as
flawlessly constructed as an origami heron, achieving at the end of
his recitation the concision of a haiku: "personal trust must tran-
scend history and culture," and, slightly more wistful, "a gentleman's agreement is fantastic if everybody is a gentleman"; Ingo
Walter, director of the Salomon Center at New York University, an
owlish man in a rumpled suit, very proud of his coining of a new
acronym, BOBs, to signify the slings and arrows of outrageous
fortune (a.k.a. "bolts out of the blue") that sometimes forced themselves upon the attention of the global economy.

Foges had described the forum's supporting cast of wandering
scholars as "the cabaret," a troupe of singing historians and dancing
economists, bearded futurists performing magic tricks with statis-
tical levitations instead of with rabbits and silk handkerchiefs, phi-
losopher clowns blowing the trumpets of doom. After only two days
in Davos I could appreciate Foges' point, but I was more attracted
to the metaphor of a medieval passion play. The corporate participants remained faithful to their program of exits and entrances,
diligent in the study of their briefing books, no less earnest than the
intellectual entertainment in their mumbling of ritual abstraction,
and I could easily picture the company dressed in ermine cloaks and

velvet hats, staging in the streets of Bayreuth or Oberammergau an annual performance of the wonderful old Easter pageant, *The Agony of Mammon.*

But neither could I fail to admire the sincerity of their devotions or the wealth of their good intentions, and as I rummaged through the notes spread across a breakfast table at an altitude of 5,000 feet, I thought of the businessmen who hadn't bothered to come to Davos, who didn't think it worth their time and trouble to make the ascent from the low-lying places of the earth, Thomas Mann's "flatlands," where men flailed at one another with stupidity and knives. In New York on the night before I left for Zurich I'd been to dinner at Le Bernadin with three principals in a successful hedge fund who characterized the Davos meeting as a futile transfer of worthless platitudes. The action in New York City during the week in question might turn up something a helluva lot more interesting than snow, and who could afford the lost opportunity cost? Why bother to dress up the everyday cruelties of standard capitalist business practice with the rags of a Sunday conscience? To what purpose, and for whose benefit? Who was anybody kidding?

One of the gentlemen at the table ordered a $2,000 bottle of Latour, in celebration of their fund's triumphant short-selling of the Japanese yen, and when they had finished with the fish, they fell to talking about the prospect of a raid on the South African krugerrand. The sizeable sums of the speculations, their own and those of like-minded investors in London or Hong Kong or Buenos Aires, undoubtedly placed heavy strains on the troubled economies of the two countries, possibly even to the point of forcing the devaluation of both currencies and bringing into play the corollary effects customarily expressed as severe unemployment, high rates of interest or inflation, large-scale distributions of misery and fear. So what? Why should they concern themselves with the crying in a foreign wilderness? Self-interest was the name of the game, and if you didn't play to win, probably you were fool enough to go to Davos.

"Fool enough," Klaus Schwab said, "or maybe wise enough to know that there are many kinds of fool, quite a few of them running governments or guns."

He had arrived promptly at 10 o'clock, a balding, blue-eyed man in his early sixties wearing a gray overcoat and a wool scarf, taller than I had expected but otherwise confirming the rumor of a hopeful professor and a chronic idealist. Before bringing up the subject of the cynicism seated at the corner table in one of New York's more expensive restaurants, I'd asked enough questions about the World Economic Forum—its origins and purpose, the qualifications for membership, the nature of its influence—to know that Schwab probably could have guessed which of the investment bankers held season tickets to the Knicks games and which one had ordered the $2,000 bottle of Latour. The professor didn't require attendance on the part of the Wall Street betting crowd, and the forum directed its efforts to those happy few among the world's enlightened capitalists, not more than one in five, who were prepared to extend their sphere of interest beyond the frontiers of a wine list.

Schwab arranged the first Davos meeting in 1971 for the benefit

of about 400 European businessmen interested in the societal defi-
nitions of the new American word "entrepreneurship." Then a professor of economics at the International Management Institute business school in Geneva, Schwab rounded up a program of speakers
knowledgeable in the ways and means of freeing commercial enterprise from the bondage of government regulation. The meeting
proved so successful that Schwab reconvened it in 1972. By 1973 it
had become the World Economic Forum and an annual event,
gradually broadening the range of its concerns and beginning to
attract important politicians and prominent businessmen from Asia
and the Americas as well as from Europe.

"Suddenly Davos was a place where they could talk to each
other," Schwab said, "all at the same time, all in the same place,
without having to travel to so many different countries, without
having to work through a lot of embassies or appointment secretar-
ies. If you can get them to sit down together, maybe something
good will happen."

Organized as a club rather than as a think tank or policy institute, the forum limits its membership to corporations supported by
cash flows of at least $1 billion a year and graced by a chairman or
chief executive officer known to take more than a passing interest in
world affairs. The annual dues come up to $20,000, and the mem-
ber corporations (their number fixed at 1,100 by the inventory of
first-class hotel rooms in Davos) may send no more than one indi-
vidual to the January conversations on the magic mountain. Every
now and then the forum revises the guest list, retiring those of its

members who, although still rich, no longer retain their place at the forefront of new technologies, new ideas. Not always an easy thing to do, shooting the old elephants, Schwab said, but how else did one stay current with the trend and temper of the times? Fifteen years ago the member corporations were mostly European, mostly banks and large-scale manufacturers; now the membership was more evenly balanced with Asian and American corporations, many of them embodying the forward-looking industries—communications, media, tourism, genetic engineering, the retail trades.

As supplements to the Davos meeting, the forum sponsors regional meetings, in Singapore or Cape Town or Washington, and Schwab had noticed that no matter what the latitude and time zone, the conversation over the last decade had been veering away from the sharply defined questions of means—How? At what price?—to a vaguely expressed questioning of ends—Why? For what purpose? He attributed the shift in emphasis to an awareness among the more thoughtful of the world's landlords that the global economy was a good deal more complicated than anybody had thought, and that in the absence of a coherent argument from the socialist left, even the most well-meaning corporate citizens found themselves marooned in a vacuum, a comfortable and well-furnished vacuum, of course, but still, unhappily, a vacuum.

It was Schwab's worry about the vacuum, intellectual as well as moral, that invited my own remark about the three bankers at Le Bernadin, which in turn prompted Schwab to mention the armed and dangerous fools disturbing the peace of nations. Somebody had

to address the problems, which was why the masters of the corporate universe had to learn how to think like statesmen, and why the
World Economic Forum provided discussions of politics and philosophy together with briefings on the bond and currency markets.

"It's no use telling these people how to become more successful,"
Schwab said. "If they didn't already know how to do that, they
wouldn't be here. They're very sure of themselves."

The wistfulness in his voice echoed the wistfulness in the voice of
Shoichiro Toyoda, and in the ensuing silence, Schwab stirring a
spoon in his coffee cup and watching two small birds chase one
another through the branches of a pine tree, I suddenly remembered
a movie made by Akira Kurosawa that I hadn't seen in twenty years.
What came as clearly into focus as the thin, unwavering lines of
smoke rising from the town of Davos was the scene in which an old
Zen monk traps a young and violent bandit in a bamboo cage,
gleefully hauling his prize into a tree as if he'd caught a wild
animal. The bandit grunts and bares his teeth; the monk laughs and
recites Zen koans. The next ten or fifteen minutes of the film en-
compass the teachings of as many years, the monk hurling Buddhist
scrolls through the bars as if they were cabbages or fresh-killed
rabbits, forcing his captive to eat from the hand of wisdom. Told as
a cautionary tale in three two-hour episodes, the movie follows the
story of the bandit changed into the chivalrous figure of a samurai
warrior who fights his last victorious duel with a wooden sword, the
weakness of his weapon transformed by the strength of his spirit.
Schwab bore as little physical resemblance to Kurosawa's monk as

he did to the medical director of Mann's sanatorium, but it wasn't hard to imagine him bombarding corporate boardrooms with philosophical e-mail messages, reminding the sometimes primitive executives to eat the bread of "globalism" and drink the milk of "dialogue."

We talked for no more than fifty minutes, Schwab fitting his remarks to the length of a college lecture, and as we descended together in the cabin of the hotel funicular with the late morning crowd of participants (freshly shaven and bright with the scent of expensive cologne, comparing notes about which of that day's sessions they planned to attend), I wondered if the World Economic Forum had discovered a means of assigning its pupils a passing or a failing grade.

Judging by my own observations of the class matriculating at Davos in the winter of 1998, it didn't seem likely that Schwab would find a surplus of honor students. Not because the lords and ladies of capitalist creation (mostly lords, not many ladies) weren't intelligent—a high percentage of them were a good deal more intelligent and considerably better informed than their analogues in the academic and literary guilds—but because they lacked the temperament for politics. They had achieved their success by virtue of their talent for organization, and they defined the dilemma of post-modern capitalism as a problem in management rather than as a search for metaphors. Their opinions largely shaped by the media that they also happened to own, they believed that the world's parliaments served at the pleasure of the world's markets, that politics was a subsidiary function of economics, and that democracy an agreeable by-product of capitalism. Legislatures came and went like football teams and fruit flies, and politicians belonged to one of only two familiar types, both untrustworthy—light-minded demagogues stirring up crowds, or "pesky legislators" constantly bothering people with demands for bribes. Markets might have their flaws, but government was worse. Ideology wrecked the free play of natural distribution, and government never knew how to manage anything—not roads, not dairy farms or gambling casinos or capital flows. All would be well, and civilization much improved, if only a healthy brand of politics (salt-free, risk-averse, baby-soft) could be manufactured in the way that one manufactured aspirin, cameras and shampoo.

The point seemed so obvious to most of the participants that when John J. Sweeney, the president of the AFL-CIO, stepped up to the podium in the Congress Hall on Saturday morning, his audience was predisposed to listen to another ten minutes of government-inspected cliché, resolute in the recognition of the "challenges" implicit in the mechanics of "economic restructuring and enterprise reform." If a Chinese communist could find his way out of the Marxist dungeon, surely an American labor leader could do the same.

But Sweeney turned out to be one of the few people at the forum willing to give public voice to the constituencies of private alarm. Like everybody else in Davos he acknowledged the feats of modern technology and the miracles of corporate production, but he failed to see how the enormous sums of new wealth had been made to serve the needs of the many as well as the pleasures of the few.

"Look around the world," he said: "Japan mired in recession, Asia in crisis ... Russia plagued by a kind of primitive, gangster capitalism, Europe stagnant, Africa largely written off ... Latin America adrift."

The straws were already blowing in the wind, and unless the profits generated by the global economy were more evenly distributed and equally shared, the nations of the earth could look forward to a siege of violence that "may make the twentieth century seem tranquil by comparison." Nor did Sweeney take much comfort in the proofs of American prosperity proclaimed by the rising prices on the New York Stock Exchange. Yes, the United States was an economic success story, and some people were doing very well indeed, but one child in four was born to poverty, the schools were in shambles and so were the hospitals and the roads, and no system succeeds, at least not for very long, if the workers cannot afford to buy what they produce. Even in America, that rich and happy land, the widening chasm between rich and poor was becoming more difficult to cross; so were the distances between the literate and the illiterate, between the freedom granted to unregulated capital and the servitude imposed on non-union labor.

"If labor has no role," Sweeney said, "democracy has no future."

The observation evoked murmurs of disagreement and an impatient rustling of programs and briefing books. A Dutch banker rose

to suggest that perhaps Mr. Sweeney hadn't been paying close attention in the conference rooms, perhaps had missed the news about
the restorative tonic of privatization sure to cure the illness of the
Asian and European economies by making them more fiercely competitive.

"What you are talking about," he said, "is protectionism, some
sort of gift to American labor."

"No," Sweeney said. "Not protectionism. A fair division of the
spoils. At the moment the workers get the austerity and little else.
The speculators get the prosperity."

Sweeney's rejoinder dropped like a pebble into a well of indiffer-
ence, and his remarks would have been dismissed without further
notice if he hadn't been followed to the podium by George Soros,
the financier as famous for his political philanthropy as he was
venerated for his vast fortune. Who could fail to heed the utterances
of George Soros, the voice of wealth incarnate and therefore omni-
scient? At Davos he was the man whom everybody wanted to see,
the saviour of Eastern Europe and the patron saint of Prague, who
had earned $1 billion in one week in 1992 by speculating against
the British pound, a quasi-mythical figure believed to have discovered Rumpelstiltskin's secret of weaving straw into gold. Sweeney's
words were of as little consequence as a scattering of sand, but
Soros's words were as heavy as the stones on Easter Island, and Soros
was as bleak as Sweeney.

Only imbeciles believed in the conscience of markets, Soros said,
imbeciles and tenured professors of economics. Markets were as

dumb as posts and as blind as bats, inherently unstable because dependent upon what people wish for, not what they have in hand, and therefore impossible to maintain in a state of equilibrium.

"Imagine a pendulum," Soros said, "a pendulum that has become a wrecking ball, swinging out of control and with increasing speed, knocking over one economy after another. First Mexico, then Indonesia and South Korea, and who knows what happens next? Maybe Brazil. Maybe Japan."

The murmuring in the Congress Hall turned suddenly apprehensive, and the pretty girls with the hand-held microphones found themselves besieged by participants wishing to offer an objection. The questions extended the remarks of the Dutch banker. What had happened to the blessings of privatization? To the infinite wisdom of the good old invisible hand?

"Market fundamentalism doesn't work," Soros said. "Without the intervention in Asia of the IMF and the World Bank, the whole system would have fallen apart."

The questions persisted until the time expired, Soros responding to them with an air of cheerful pessimism. Left to its own devices, he said, the global market undoubtedly would destroy itself. Not for any ideological reason, not because it resented rich people or failed to vote Republican, but because it obeyed the laws of motion rather than the rule of reason, and it didn't know how to do anything else except destroy itself. Certainly it would be nice if somebody could invent a set of international institutions capable of restraining the market, maybe something in the spirit of the old

Bretton Woods agreement or along the lines of a Federal Reserve System. When economic catastrophes are "big enough to stop the music," Soros said, one needs a mechanism "to restart the lending." Several people rose to ask about the precise nature of the mechanism, wondering how the international institutions might be constructed, and from whom or whence they would derive the patents of authority. Soros smiled and didn't know the answers, and when the plenary session ended in what was still a clamor of anxious voices, he abandoned the company to its further investigations and bid them all a fond farewell.

The speeches and briefing sessions continued for another three days, but to the best of my knowledge nobody found a secret computer password, at least none that was posted on any electronic message board, solving the riddle of the global economy or justifying the market's ways to man. It wasn't that the participants didn't look. God knows, they looked—peering at documents, attentive to the simultaneous translations in Russian and Japanese, steadfast in their consumption of the plum brandy—but they never managed to discover the binding formulas of advanced technology that could invest Leviathan with a Christian conscience or a human face. The variables were too many and too hard to calculate, and even if they could be reduced to well-behaved rows of digital code, the printouts coming back from the Congress Centre's computers presumably would read like the ones issued by the fortune-telling machine in a penny arcade—sell gold, buy Islam, be home before midnight, and don't play Monopoly with Japanese banks.

Several prominent participants, most of them American, offered miracle cures and magic remedies, and on Sunday morning Newt Gingrich, the Speaker of the House of Representatives, appeared before the club of media leaders in the Post Stubi in the Posthotel, resplendent in his song-and-dance-man's character of the man who knows too much. At ease in the thin, upland atmospheres of inspired cliché and genially dismissive of the doubts that troubled the common herd of lesser men, Gingrich boasted of America's unparalleled place in the world—its possession of supreme military and economic power, its immense spending for scientific research, its unquestionable capacity to shelter the nations of the earth under the eagles of what Gingrich called "the *Pax Humana*," a phrase and a concept he thought more faithful to the geopolitical facts than the previous "*Pax Americana*," which carried with it the old, outmoded connotations of brutality and greed. From this time forward the nations of the earth should be encouraged to think themselves privileged members of a "polycentric, multipolar paradigm," rather than mere inhabitants of the unsanitary and sometimes dangerous slum once known, much too simply, as the world.

Gingrich departed in a bustle of self-importance, and the company moved into the adjacent Carieget to listen to Bill Gates, the richest man in Christendom and therefore an oracle competent to dispute, with a second and preferably more hopeful opinion, the judgment of Soros. The journalists crowded into the room as if they were shepherds come to behold the miracle at Bethlehem, and it was left to David Gergen, once a speechwriter for Presidents Richard Nixon and Ronald Reagan, to utter an appropriate word of praise: "Your name, sir, is already synonymous with the twenty-first century." But although Gates brimmed with buoyant optimism, speaking in a high, piping voice and bestowing on the company the boyish smile that graced his television endorsements for Callaway golf clubs, he lacked a reassuring aura of *gravitas*. He mentioned the "big ideas" looming just below the horizon of the millennium, and he described some of the "neat stuff" being assembled back home in the suburbs of Seattle by the genies in the bottle of Microsoft, but the impression was that of a precocious child armed with a set of Star Wars dolls.

The next day I left for Zurich, traveling by car instead of train because the journey was not as long and the wide turns in the road enlarged the view of the Grison Alps. Still in company with the canvas shoulder bag and its heavily increased weight of supplementary data, I looked for documents that I could leave conveniently behind, also for the stray observation that might suggest a summary paragraph or a last word. None was immediately forthcoming. At the end as at the beginning, I was still where Foges had found me in the bar at the Rinaldi Hotel, undoubtedly missing the point, certain that something more important had been happening somewhere else.

But neither had Foges been wrong about the number of participants wandering around as if lost or temporarily misplaced, or about the general sense of uneasiness, palpable but somehow weightless, drifting through the smoke-free atmospheres of the

Congress Centre. Among the miscellaneous papers spread across the back seat of the car I came across a surprising number of marginal remarks attributed to business as well as media leaders that drew comparisons between the global economy and the *Titanic*—references to the band on the boat deck playing the theme from *The Lion King,* jokes about the emerging market in icebergs somewhere off the starboard bow. Other notes in other briefing books recalled the wistful, almost elegiac, tone that I'd heard in the voices of Shoichiro Toyoda and Professor Schwab, and in a few barely legible lines on an envelope I again encountered the gentleman from Kenya standing in the Congress Hall, very erect and very black, to remind the distinguished panel seated on the dais that in Africa the economic news was far from good, saying of his fellow Africans—not only in Kenya, but also in Rwanda, Nigeria, Zaire—"Don't forget us ... we are here ... we are a sleeping lion."

The members of the distinguished panel, American and European bankers who had been discussing the finer points of currency speculation, clearly didn't know much about lions, sleeping or awake, and after looking at one another for a few moments in hope of a helpful comment, they passed silently on to the next question, the expressions in their faces as empty as the deserts of the Sudan. I couldn't tell whether they were embarrassed or merely irritated, but their instinctive shying away from the prospect of catastrophe spoke, more eloquently than all the forum's briefing papers, to the nature of the dilemma placed before the splendid company assembled on a majestic alp in Davos. They were a parliament of managers, and Africa was beyond the pale of management; so were most of the other global propositions (terrorism, environmental degradation, ignorance, and war) brought to the podium in the Congress Hall with the pomp and fanfare of simultaneous translation and overhead projection.

How then were the participants to proceed? They wished to live in a world governed by clearly established rules: rules of contract, rules about the transfers of money and information, rules about the polluting of rivers and politicians. The exact wording of the rules mattered less than a willingness among the interested parties to obey the same rules. A polite thought and an admirable sentiment, but if the men of Davos didn't make the rules, who would? The men of Davos didn't know. They were managers, not the kind of people given to making rules—or laws, or revolutions, or moral codes, which tumbled into the world in a mess of blood and noise, torn untimely from the womb of the status quo.

But where was the comfort in the theory of a universe bound only by the rules of profit and loss? And if the wealth of nations came and went at the pleasure of the "free market," in many ways great and glorious but in other ways as mindless as a ballbearing, then what happened to the fond belief that it was the corporate magi on the magic mountain who controlled the engine of the global economy and not the other way around? How did they escape the thought that even they, the men of Davos, danced like red-hatted monkeys to an organ grinder's merry, witless tune?

The questions didn't invite attractive answers, didn't fluff up the pillows of self-congratulation, and so the men of Davos awaited a miracle born of a foundation grant and revealed as a wonder of high technology, in the meantime holding fast to their dream of virtual government in which careful adjustments made by the geneticists and Nobel physicists in their midst transformed the wayward and ferocious energy of the world's markets into a play of light on a computer screen.

Coda

I hope we shall crush in its birth the aristocracy
of our moneyed corporations, which dare already to challenge
our government to a trial of strength and bid defiance
to the laws of our country.
— THOMAS JEFFERSON

The Davos meeting adjourned on February 3, and those of its participants called upon to issue statements or publish reports seconded the motions of hedged optimism proposed by Chancellor Kohl and Speaker Gingrich. As subscribers to the doctrines of consensus they were happy to say that crisis had been averted, that by and large and most things considered, the global economy had weathered the storm of the Asian currency devaluations, had recovered its composure in Russia, was looking brightly forward not only to the birth of the euro but also to the prospect of stability in Nigeria, prosperity in Italy, equilib-

rium in Brazil. Certain difficulties, of course, remained. Saddam
Hussein still possessed weapons of mass destruction, the Israelis and
the Palestinians were letting the milk of dialogue stand too long in
the sun, and the Japanese banks, stubbornly refusing the program of
healthy financial exercise recommended by the therapists at the
IMF, continued to confuse the arts of accounting with the symbolic
movements of the Kabuki theater. But prices were moving firmly
up on the American stock exchanges, most of the new numbers
admitted to membership on the world's computer screens glowed
with the sheen of transparency, and for the time being it was probably safe to buy resort hotels in southern Spain.

A similarly confident vocabulary and tone of voice characterized
the more detailed analysis gradually making its way down from the
magic mountain during the month of February. Markets continued
to rally in Tokyo and Hong Kong, and all appeared to be well in the
polycentric, multipolar paradigm until late March, when one of
Ingo Walter's BOBs interrupted the nightly news from Moscow.
Very suddenly and without the courtesy of prior rumor, Boris Yeltsin dismissed Viktor Chernomyrdin, the Russian prime minister
whom I had last seen in the Congress Centre's Sanada Room, telling
his capitalist friends (his very good capitalist friends) that all the
economic weather vanes in Russia were pointing due west into the
fair wind of the free market—wonderful statistics, the army being
paid, risks reduced and the ruble gaining strength, inflation a dim
memory, massive inducements to foreign capital, everybody singing
songs. Apparently the wind had stopped blowing. It wasn't only

Chernomyrdin who had been summarily removed; so had all the other members of the cabinet, and the new staff of government ministers didn't look like people apt to inspire the confidence of the concierge at the Berghotel Schatzalp.

Meanwhile, in Indonesia the natives were becoming distinctly restless, the newspapers reporting riots in the town of Kroton and the city of Surabaya, troops deployed in the suburbs of Djakarta, students burning flags. General Suharto needed the $10 billion consigned to the rescue of the rupiah by the emissaries of the IMF, but the terms of the loan weren't winning a vote of gratitude from a population required to pay wholesome, free-market prices for gasoline and food. Unable to afford the cost of what the bankers deemed a proper show of austerity, most everybody in Indonesia had been reduced to eating insects.

The rioting quickened in intensity throughout the month of April—downtown Djakarta put to the torch, IMF officials departing on a chartered plane, looters in the megamalls ransacking Wal-Mart, Dunkin' Donuts and Pizza Hut, rich Chinese merchants so frightened of the mob that they were attempting to rent a column of tanks—and on May 21, the rupiah having lost another 20 percent of its value in almost as many days, Suharto at last resigned.

May was a banner month for BOBs in both the Northern and Southern Hemispheres—South Korea reporting unpaid wages of $334 million, Russia paying interest rates of 100 percent to buyers of its government debt—but none was more contrary to the picture-postcard "outlooks" on the future distributed to the winter tourists at Davos than the Indian thermonuclear initiative. The underground explosions in the Rajasthan desert on May 11 not only spoiled the forum's snapshot of warm and welcoming Bombay ("Session Number 164, India: Sustaining Economic Growth and the Pace of Reform"), they also called into question the forum's faith in the wonders of high technology. The tests took the American CIA entirely by surprise, the failure of intelligence explained by the agency's having placed too much trust in its electronics and map overlays, and if even the CIA couldn't teach its satellites to think, what then happened to the greater hope of a virtual government elected by a vote of informed semiconductors?

Further refutations of the lesson preached at Davos showed up in the frenzy of mergers and acquisitions that ravaged the provinces of corporate empire throughout the spring and early summer. Which was not at all what one might have expected had one been listening to the apostles of the "new information order" roaming around the Congress Centre like a brotherhood of chanting monks. Visionary and insistent, they never tired of drawing diagrams on paper napkins, handing out high-speed paradigms, promoting the virtues inherent in the cellular forms of enterprise. Now that the Cold War was over, what was the use of "Big Brother," "big government," "big business"? The spirit of the times was said to be moving off in less monolithic directions, away from top-heavy tables of organization toward the smaller fonts of energy and intellect convenient to the play of mind.

The corporate laity listened with the rapture of new believers, sometimes volunteering a text or vision of their own, praising Jesus or the elves of Silicon Valley for the miracles of flex-time and the microchip. Their enthusiasm didn't survive their return to lower altitudes. Back home in Connecticut or Michigan they once again embraced the great and golden truth that size matters, that big is beautiful, and biggest best of all. Within the span of a few excited days in late April and early May, Daimler-Benz acquired Chrysler, NationsBank merged with BankAmerica, and Citicorp pooled its assets with Traveler's Group in a deal priced at $140 billion. By mid-May *The New York Times* was reporting the aggregate sum of the year's 444 announced mergers and/or acquisitions at $630 billion (against the mere $260 billion assembled during the first five months of 1997), and in Washington the House of Representatives had passed a bill meant to assist the making of monopolies.

The building of enormous fortifications follows from the holding of correspondingly large portfolios of fear, and the mammoth size of the newly formed companies suggested accumulations of dread measured on the scale of the Great Wall of China. Trailing well behind the front-page stories (the richest this, the biggest that), the newspapers sometimes came upon a discreet but unnamed source explaining that the brave new merger proceeded from a siege of panic. Yes, the Cold War had come safely to an end, and yes, the deregulation of the global economy had bestowed upon the consuming public any number of precious boons; but the new economic order had also spawned the birth of monsters rising like Godzilla from the sea of alien debt, and how was a company supposed to stay in business, much less afford what Professor Schwab would recognize as a decent global presence, unless it transformed itself into one of those heavy robots, mechanical and all-devouring, that clank across the landscape of a George Lucas movie?

The executives who proudly unveiled the new and improved corporate logo for the cameras in the hotel ballroom tactfully omitted any references to apocalypse. If they suspected the imminent and unwelcome arrival of a new round of BOBs—steadily falling prices paid for oil and steel, stores of unsold wheat rising like Egyptian pyramids on the Dakota plains, too many of Ralph Lauren's polo shirts decorating the warehouses in Canton—they didn't share the information with the stockholders or the financial press. But neither did they cast their remarks in the language of the Davos enlightenment; neglecting to reaffirm their faith in progress, their trust in human reason, or their belief in the wisdom of John Maynard Keynes, they left it to the more perceptive investors in the ballroom to find the message in the fortune cookie of what they didn't say. Perhaps the global markets had become too closely intertwined, the safety of the whole too easily threatened by the whim or weakness of any of the parts. Who then could afford to take chances with an undernourished politician or an overvalued baht?

The month of August settled the questions in favor of panic and retreat. Terrorist bombs destroyed the American embassies in Kenya and Tanzania on August 7, and within the narrow compass of the next twenty-four days Iraq suspended the UN arms inspections, calamitous flooding in China (on the amiable Mr. Li's rivers of austerity) forced the evacuation of 13 million people and the abandonment of 5 million dwellings, civil war in the former Yugoslavia chased 200,000 Kosovars into starvation or the forest, President Clinton castrated the office of the American presidency by conceding his "inappropriate relationship" with Monica Lewinsky, a car bomb killed twenty-eight people in Northern Ireland, American cruise missiles obliterated a barracks in Afghanistan and a chemical factory in Khartoum (the bombing limited to Mr. Richardson's category of "pinprick," not yet "substantial" or "massive"), Malaysia removed its currency from the international trading pit, the Russian economy collapsed (what little was left of Yeltsin's government devaluing the ruble and suspending repayment of its foreign debt), and the Dow Jones Industrial Average suffered a loss in value amounting to $297 billion.

By the first week in September the US State Department was advising its dependents to flee their embassies in Albania, Pakistan, East Africa and the Congo, and the accountants picking through the ruins of the Russian economy noticed that George Soros hadn't managed to get out of the way of his own wrecking ball. Soros's Quantum Fund had lost $2 billion of its investment in the illusion of a sturdy ruble, and if even the Great Kahn Soros could make so costly a mistake, then who was God and where was heaven? The free market didn't know, and prices on the world's stock exchanges staggered up and down the indices in search of answers to questions that the computers couldn't frame in words. The news media buzzed with theories and explanations, many of them supplied to

MSNBC and the op-ed page of *The Wall Street Journal* by the same expert witnesses who had entertained the company in Davos. Their commentary recapitulated the sotto voce uneasiness that I'd encountered between briefing sessions in the Congress Hall, an uneasiness become more audible because associated with a sequence of events but still somehow weightless, still drifting in what Klaus Schwab had characterized as a moral and intellectual vacuum.

Historians presented analogies, politicians expressed hopes, economists recommended policies, moralists passed judgments, but their collective wisdom amounted to little more than a sending of signals in smoke. No government possessed the authority to correct the global economy's failed math exam; no government, no set of international institutions or agreements, no council of seers seated in one of the UN's handsome buildings in Geneva, no committee in Brussels, no bank in Frankfurt, least of all the self-defeated leaders of the United States, Russia and Japan. Which left matters in the hands of Alan Greenspan, the chairman of the Federal Reserve Board, who was hastily outfitted with powers and divinities not unlike those once awarded to a Roman consul leaving for the wars against Hannibal and the Carthaginian elephants. Mindful of the urgency of the task in hand, the chairman delivered an uncharacteristically forthright speech at the University of California on September 5, drawing the attention of his audience to the great truth of the great platitude about the nature of the geo-economic order in the post-modern world.

"It is just not credible," he said, "that the United States can remain an oasis of prosperity unaffected by a world that is experiencing greatly increased stress."

The financial markets interpreted the chairman's remark as a sign that the Federal Reserve meant to lower American interest rates, and stock prices the next day floated briefly upwards on a spasm of general rejoicing. The chairman didn't make as heroic an impression on Kiichi Miyazawa, the Japanese finance minister with whom he had dinner in San Francisco on the same day that he spoke to the students in Berkeley. Minister Miyazawa objected to the naming of Japan as Public Enemy Number One and the last seven years of Tokyo's financial mismanagement being blamed for the economic wreckage on four continents, and he left the dinner table with what was reported as a noticeable reluctance to bow before the majesty of the American Rome. Noble Greenspan returned to Washington without a victory and no procession of captured auditors or enslaved currency speculators, but he was applauded in the Capitol for his patriotic zeal, and the newspapers were loud with voices rallying to the standards of transparency and thrift. Robert Rubin, the secretary of the treasury, observed that "the number of countries experiencing difficulties at once is something we have not seen before … an unprecedented situation in a host of respects"; Michel Camdessus, managing director of the IMF, acknowledged the danger of a situation "by far not fully rational."

Neither Secretary Rubin nor Managing Director Camdessus had foreseen the consequences of what they had regarded as their judicious lending to the less favored nations of the earth—Camdessus declaring Russia preserved from crisis as recently as early July, Rubin amazed to discover how little the New York banks and mutual funds knew about the nature of their investments in Asia—but now that trouble had come so close to the American shore they could see, as if with the eyes of little children, that the world was short of cash. Too much product on the markets, and not enough money in the hands of people willing and able to buy another Japanese motorcycle, another Armani suit, another bottle of Latour.

For the next two weeks the news media kept up the drumroll of impending doom—more Japanese banks declared insolvent, stronger rumors of "global recession," a torrent of nervous money flooding into the United States bond market from every quarter of the globe—and then on Monday, September 21, the mountain came to Mammon, and the spirit of Davos descended on the island of Manhattan in the cloud of an all-day seminar graced by the presence of President and Hillary Clinton. The World Economic Forum didn't lend its auspices to the occasion, but the title of the program ("Strengthening Democracy in the Global Economy: An Opening Dialogue") could have been composed by Klaus Schwab himself, and the proceedings at the New York University School of Law were carried forward in the proper atmosphere of high-altitude abstraction. The guests assembled in a handsomely wainscotted room on Washington Square, among them John Sweeney and the director of the London School of Economics, were appropriately distinguished; the media leaders in attendance supplied a flattering sense of significant event, and the panelists seated at a polished library table around a centerpiece of cut flowers exchanged the customary gifts of exquisite euphemism—capitalism encouraged to show a human face, urgent need to shift assets from short-term speculation to long-term value, general lack of civic responsibility, incalculable damage to the environment, urgent need for new financial architecture built to the specifications of the new Information Age, fear of contagion in Brazil, transparency still in short supply, multinational morality a must, urgent need for Science! Technology! Education! Engineers!

The steady drone of sonorous banality blurred into a sound not unlike the murmur of contented bees, and because it was hard to stay awake, much less take responsible notes, I almost missed the one remark on the program that might have provoked a lively conversation. About 3 o'clock in the afternoon the panelists reached the question of transparency in Asia, the appalling lack of it attributed to poor market supervision (a shortfall of regulatory agencies, not enough data in the computers, inadequate means of democratic oversight, etc.), and when somebody unexpectedly paused to consult a note, Laura Tyson, the former chairperson of President Clinton's Council of Economic Advisers, interrupted the discussion to observe that the heavy capital flows that had drowned the Asian economies didn't come from Asia. They came from Europe and the United States, from fully developed industrial countries well-equipped with sufficient data and the instruments of democratic oversight. What we are talking about here, she said, is greed ... stupidity, cowardice and greed ... about investors in London and

Paris and New York seizing the prey of easy profits and then, when the luck went bad, seeking to transfer their markers to a government ... about privatizing the gains, socializing the losses.

The distinguished company didn't pursue Ms. Tyson's line of argument. A gentleman associated with Goldman, Sachs coughed discreetly into his microphone, Hillary Clinton smiled at a television camera, two media leaders adjusted their very attractive ties. The murmuring resumed, and I didn't again pick up the trend of the conversation until 4:30 when President Clinton walked into the room with a swarm of photographers.

For the president, it hadn't been a happy day. Beginning about 10 a.m. the networks had been broadcasting his grand-jury testimony in the matter of Monica Lewinsky—all four hours of the unedited videotape—and it was still too soon to guess at the response of the opinion polls. The guests in the law school library expressed their sympathy with an enthusiastic welcome of sustained applause. The president acknowledged the courtesy with a wan smile, introduced the three other participants on his panel (the prime minister of Italy, the president of Bulgaria, "my good friend Tony Blair") and deftly forestalled the possibility of further embarrassment by escaping into his character as the country's supreme policy expert—the senior lecturer come to explicate a famous but ambiguous text (i.e., *The Wealth and Poverty of Nations*) for a class of attentive graduate students.

The president spoke for the better part of two hours, playing the double roles of moderator and principal participant, drawing the distinction between "internationalists" and "isolationists," favoring "mega-choices" and "micro-loans," endorsing the wisdom of the Noble Greenspan ("America is not immune! … We cannot remain an island of prosperity in a sea of despair!"), recommending wide distribution of "the tools of empowerment," calling for "fresh perspectives" and ending with a well-told homily about the importance of global warming.

It was an impressive recitation made more impressive by the circumstances in which it was performed, but as I listened to the president speak, his display of utmost concern precisely matched to the current measure of public alarm, I began to understand (more clearly than I had understood in Davos), the point of Klaus Schwab's remark about the corporate oligarchy being marooned in a vacuum. Here was the president of the United States addressing the prospect of worldwide recession with nothing other than an empty set of abstractions and no weight of authority—moral, intellectual, political or spiritual—that might inform his words with meaning and force. His fine pose of high presidential seriousness was exactly that—a pose, an extended television commercial, a department store window display. By his own all too recent admission, his words were counterfeit, made, like his presidency, to be seen and not heard. The judgment of the next day's opinion polls counted for as little as the House Judiciary Committee's deciding whether or not to proceed to an impeachment hearing. Clinton already had been impeached—impeached long before his enemies hobbled him with the thongs of Monica Lewinsky's red satin underwear, im-

peached before he served his first term in office, impeached as a
prior condition to his being given the money with which to mount
an election campaign.

Despite Clinton's sometimes picturesque rhetoric to the contrary, he always had been a politician who could be relied upon not
to quarrel with the selfishness of the geo-economic theory that now
suddenly threatened to demonstrate the downside of its nature in
American as well as Asian grocery stores, and the longer I listened
to him talk, the more easily I could imagine him in the Davos
cabaret—strutting the year-end numbers, juggling the projections,
glad to accept the premise that democracy was a public-affairs program made possible by a grant from the corporate sponsors. He had
as little notion of how to get out of the way of George Soros's
wrecking ball as did George Soros, and his bewilderment was a
measure of the extent to which what Jefferson once called "the
aristocracy of our moneyed corporations" had crushed the country's
political spirit.

The seminar concluded with a farewell round of long applause—for Hillary's impressive show of strength in the face of
scandal as well as for the president's lecture on global economics—and among the participants pushing toward the doors, I
looked for Ingo Walter, the director of the Salomon Center at NYU
who had coined the acronym BOBs. I remembered that at Davos he
had also said something about how bank managers were supposed
to perform "a function similar to that of a zoo keeper, managing
wild animals," and I wanted to ask him how so many of the animals

had escaped from their cages. Where would they be going next, the animals, and on whom would they be feeding? I couldn't find Walter in the crowd, but in Washington Square I came across two gentlemen seated on a bench and dressed in garbage bags, talking to themselves in what I took to be an illegal dream of heaven, and I couldn't help but notice that the grins on their faces were not less fixed or distant than those on the faces of the participants in the law school library, sucking at the straws of dialogue.

Glossary

An abbreviated list of meanings assigned to words in common use at Davos and other international conferences.

AUSTERITY

Healthy and invigorating program of fiscal exercise for people who cannot afford to go to business school. Constant practice encourages a sober respect for the value of money.

BAILOUT

Difficult word because its two contrary meanings depend solely on the context. Thus A, with reference to somebody else's investments, a criminal fraud perpetrated by corrupt banks and lying politicians. Or B, with reference to one's own investment, a just reward bestowed upon a courageous entrepreneur.

BOSNIA

Tragic story.

BUDGET REFORM

Noble cause. Ronald Reagan believed in it; so did Margaret Thatcher and Charles de Gaulle. The phrase doesn't lend itself to literal translation in any of the Asian languages.

BUREAUCRATS

Enemies of Free Enterprise. No bureaucrat knows what it means to meet a payroll or take a risk. Europe has too many of them.

CAMPAIGN SLOGANS

Political equivalents of junk bonds.

CEOs

Champions of the people, heroes of our time. Their clarity of mind allows them to subtract 40,000 superfluous workers without a moment's qualm or hesitation.

CIVIL LIBERTIES

Favors granted to minorities, criminals, radicals, and the undeserving poor. Extremely expensive.

CONSENSUS

Always preferable to argument. It speaks in a voice not unlike that of the concierge in a first-class hotel.

CONTAGION

Never a pretty sight. Currencies infected with the disease turn brown at the corners and brittle on the edges.

CORPORATION, TRANSNATIONAL

Late-twentieth-century institution comparable to the medieval Church or the legions of ancient Rome. Because it exists in the realm of pure abstraction it can give birth to its own parents.

CORRUPTION

Sign of a mature society. The practice of offering and accepting bribes teaches the lesson of civility.

CULTURE

Fancy name for traditional costumes worn by schoolchildren on public holidays.

DEMOCRACY

Outworn system of government unequal to the challenges of the twenty-first century.

DIALOGUE

Life-giving elixir administered in large quantities to people too poor to buy Prozac or cocaine.

DICTATORS

They know their own minds. Often easier to deal with than elected legislatures.

ECONOMIC SOVEREIGNTY

Entrusted to corporations, not governments. The world's parliaments serve at the pleasure of the world's markets.

EMERGING MARKETS

Similar to striptease clubs and Hungarian cab drivers. They must be approached with caution.

ETHICS

Native handicrafts. The best ones are made of soapstone, ivory and sandalwood.

FASCISM

A much happier and more efficient system of government than is generally supposed. Hitler gave it a bad name.

FREE MARKET

The few people who still question its omniscience belong to weird religious sects.

FUR COAT

Symbol of democracy.

GLOBAL ECONOMY

Wonderfully ornate mechanism engineered by wise financiers to guarantee the happiness of mankind. It requires the participation of investors instead of citizens.

GOVERNMENT REGULATION

Similar to serpents or vines. It strangles the sinews of industry.

HAITI

Tragic story.

HISTORY

Ended happily in 1989.

IDEALISM

Dangerous substance. If left standing too long at room temperature on a library table, idealism congeals into ideology, which breeds totalitarianism and puritanical reigns of virtue. Robespierre was an idealist. So was Lenin.

INTEGRATIONISTS

Forward-looking and sophisticated people who recognize the inevitability of the global economy and appreciate the distinction between the Mouton-Rothschild and the Cordeillan-Bages.

INTERNATIONAL MONETARY FUND

It doesn't have enough money to buy France, much less run the world.

LEFT-BEHINDS, THE

Backward and fearful people who don't know how to operate computers. They lead sad lives and usually die before reaching the age of sixty.

MCDONALD'S

Symbol of democracy.

MINIMUM CONSENSUS PROGRAM

Terms under which a government surrenders its sovereignty to a consortium of banks.

MONEY

The light of the world and the mandate of Heaven.

MONOPOLY

Glorious manifestation of human ingenuity. The source of all our blessings.

MULTICULTURALISM

The department stores understand it better than the universities.

NATIONALISM

Last refuge of small and impoverished countries without a well-developed tourist trade. Instead of tennis courts and boat marinas they offer street riots and recreational looting.

OVERCAPACITY

The ruin of us all.

POLITICIANS

They used to be made of marble; now they are made of straw.

POOR, THE

Inspirational by-products of the global economy. They perform a necessary service, reminding people more fortunately placed that civilization entails sacrifice.

PROFITS

Never indecent or obscene.

REDUCED LABOR COSTS

An ingredient necessary to the making of good plum cake.

RWANDA

Tragic story.

SMITH, ADAM

Great man. The eighteenth-century avatar of Bill Gates.

TECHNOLOGY

Indispensable. Hard to remember how one got along without it.

TERRORISTS

The most dangerous ones come from good families.

TITANIC, THE

Famous ship. Foolish people compare it to the global economy.

TRANSPARENCY

Worth its weight in gold.

UNEMPLOYMENT

Necessary check on inflation.

WARS

The only important ones involve large corporations, not nation-states.

Appendix

An incomplete but representative roster of participants (listed alphabetically) at the Davos meeting of the World Economic Forum, January 29–February 3, 1998.

Corporate Executives

Alireza, Khalid A., *Chairman,* Saudi Cable Company,
   Saudi Arabia
Argüden, Yilmaz, *Chairman,* Erdemir, **Turkey**
Bhaskaran, Manu, *Director,* Socgen-Crosby Securities,
   Singapore
Chan, Ronnie C., *Chairman,* Hang Lung Development Company Limited, **Hong Kong**
Gates, William H. III, *Chairman and Chief Executive Officer,*
   Microsoft Corporation, **USA**
Herkströter, Cor A.J., *Chairman,* Royal Dutch/Shell, **Netherlands**
Holliday, Shaun, *Managing Director,* Guinness Ireland Group,
   Ireland

Idei, Nobuyuki, *President and Representative Director,* Sony Corporation,
  Japan
Jing Shuping, *Chairman,* All-China Federation of Industry and
  Commerce, China
Lindahl, Göran, *President and Chief Executive Officer,* ABB Asea Brown
  Boveri Ltd., Switzerland
Maughan, Deryck C., *Co-Chairman and Co-Chief Executive Officer,* Salomon
  Smith Barney, USA
Monod, Jérôme, *Chairman of the Supervisory Board,* Suez-Lyonnaise Des
  Eaux, France
Naki, Nasser, *Vice-Chairman,* Arabian Light Metals KSC, Kuwait
Orsi, Vittorio, *Chairman of the Board,* Scac Fundaçoes e Estruturas Ltda.,
  Brazil
Piëch, Ferdinand, *Chairman of the Board of Management,* Volkswagen AG,
  Germany
Piramal, Ajay G., *Chairman,* Piramal Enterprises Limited, India
Romulo, Roberto R., *Chairman,* Philippine Long Distance Telephone
  Company, Philippines
Soros, George, *Chairman,* Soros Fund Management, USA
Sutherland, Peter D., *Chairman and Managing Director,* Goldman, Sachs
  International, UK
Toyoda, Shoichiro, *Chairman,* Toyota Motor Corporation, Japan

Government Officials, Elected Politicians

Ahluwalia, Montek Singh, *Secretary for Economy and Finance of India,* India
Akayev, Askar, *President of Kyrgyzstan,* Kyrgyzstan
Azoulay, Andre, *Counsellor to His Majesty King Hassan II of Morocco,*
  Morocco
Ballivian, Amparo, *Vice-Minister of Investment and Privatization of Bolivia,*
  Bolivia
Barre, Raymond, *Mayor of Lyon; Prime Minister of France, 1976–81,* France
Bildt, Carl, *Chairman of the Moderate Party,* Sweden
Byanyima, Winnie, *Member of Parliament,* Uganda
Chernomyrdin, Viktor, *Prime Minister of Russia,* Russia

Downer, Alexander, *Minister for Foreign Affairs of Australia,*
   Australia
Gingrich, Newt, *Speaker of the US House of Representatives,* **USA**
Kharrazi, Kamal, *Minister of Foreign Affairs of the Islamic Republic of Iran,*
   Iran
Kohl, Helmut, *Federal Chancellor of Germany,* **Germany**
Li Lanqing, *Vice-Premier of the People's Republic of China,* **China**
Mbeki, Thabo, *Executive Deputy President of South Africa,* **South Africa**
Menem, Carlos Saul, *President of Argentina,* **Argentina**
Sakakibara, Eisuke, *Vice-Minister of Finance for International Affairs of Ja-*
   pan, **Japan**
Santer, Jacques, *President of the European Commission, Brussels,* **EC**
Sweeney, John J., *President,* American Federation of Labor and Congress of
   Industrial Organizations (AFL-CIO), **USA**
You, Jong-Keun, *Chief Economic Policy Adviser to the President-elect of the*
   Republic of Korea, **Korea**
Zedillo Ponce de Leon, Ernesto, *President of Mexico,* **Mexico**

News Media

Auletta, Ken, *Communications Columnist,* The New Yorker, **USA**
Aleksandrowicz, Piotr, *Editor-in-Chief,* Rzeczpspolita, **Poland**
de Andrade, Sérgio, *Editor-in-Chief,* Journal de Noticias, **Portugal**
Bartley, Robert, *Editor,* The Wall Street Journal, **USA**
Bergström, Hans, *Editor-in-Chief,* Dagens Nyheter, **Sweden**
Carrubba, Salvatore, *Group Managing Editor,* Il Sole 24 Ore, **Italy**
Ceberio, Jesus, *Editor-in-Chief,* El Pais, **Spain**
Fenby, Jonathan, *Editor,* South China Morning Post, **Hong Kong**
Foges, Peter H., *Executive Producer,* Adam Smith's Money World, **USA**
Gergen, David R., *Editor-at-Large,* US News & World Report, **USA**
Izraelewicz, Erik, *Editor-in-Chief*, Le Monde, **France**
Jones, James A., *Editor-in-Chief*, Business Day, **South Africa**
Kaplan, Robert D., *Author and Contributing Editor,* The Atlantic Monthly,
   USA
Kojima, Akira, *Chief Editor*, Nikkei-Nihon Keizai Shimbun, **Japan**

Pietila, Antti-Pekka, *Senior Editor-in-Chief,* Taloussanomat, **Finland**
Pushkov, Alexei, *Director of Foreign Affairs,* Russian Public Television
  (ORT), **Russia**
Quiring, Holger, *Chief Editor,* Vereinigte Wirtschaftsdienste, **Germany**
Safire, William, *Columnist,* The New York Times, **USA**
Sarkar, Aveek, *Editor-in-Chief,* Ananda Bazar Patrika, **India**
Selman, Elias A., *Director,* Revista America Economia, **Chile**

Bankers

Ackermann, Josef, *Member of the Board of Managing Directors,* Deutsche
  Bank AG, **Germany**
Akisik, Vural, *Chief Executive Officer,* Turk Dis Ticaret Bankasi As (DIS-
  BANK), **Turkey**
Alweendo, Tom, *Governor,* Bank of Namibia, **Namibia**
Aziz, Shaukat, *Director,* Saudi American Bank (SAMBA), USA, **Pakistan**
Blum, Georges, *Chairman of the Board,* Swiss Bank Corporation,
  Switzerland
Courtis, Kenneth S., *Chief Economist and Strategist,* Deutsche Bank Group
  Asia Pacific, **Japan**
Downe, William A., *Executive Vice-President,* Global Corporate Banking,
  Bank of Montreal, **Canada**
Frenkel, Jacob A., *Governor,* Bank of Israel, **Israel**
Källäker, Håkan, *Executive Vice-President and Head, Swedbank Markets,*
  Foreningssparbanken AB (Swedbank), **Sweden**
Kohlhaussen, Martin, *Chairman of the Board of Management,* Commerz-
  bank AG, **Germany**
Kostrzewa, Wojciech J., *First Deputy President,* BRE Bank SA, **Poland**
Lipp, Ernst-Moritz, *Member of the Board of Managing Directors,* Dresdner
  Bank AG, **Germany**
Ng Thow Hing, Mary, *Group Divisional Leader,* State Bank of Mauritius
  Limited, **Mauritius**
Nourbakhsh, Mohsen, *Governor,* Central Bank of the Islamic Republic of
  Iran, **Iran**
Roubstov, Alexander, *Deputy Chairman of the Board,* National Reserve

Bank, **Russia**

Stiglitz, Joseph E., *Senior Vice-President,* World Bank, **USA**

Trichet, Jean-Claude, *Governor,* Bank of France, **France**

Wanless, Derek, *Group Chief Executive,* National Westminster Bank, **UK**

Ward, John A., *Chairman and Chief Executive Officer,* American Express Bank, **USA**

Expert Witnesses, Miscellaneous Intellectuals

Achleitner, Ann-Kristin, *Professor of Banking and Finance,* European Business School, **Germany**

Albats, Yevgenia M., *Author of* The Jewish Question *and* The State Within a State: KGB and Its Hold on Russia, **Russia**

Baginda, Abdul Razak Abdullah, *Executive Director,* Malaysian Strategic Research Centre, **Malaysia**

Boorstin, Daniel J., *Librarian Emeritus,* Library of Congress, **USA**

Dornbusch, Rudi, *Professor of Economics,* Massachusetts Institute of Technology, **USA**

Lo Hang Lap, Raymond, *Feng Shui Expert*, **Hong Kong**

Maull, Hanns W., *Professor of International Relations and Political Science,* University of Trier, **Germany**

Mernissi, Fatima, *Professor of Sociology,* Université Mohammed V, **Morocco**

Mohan, Rakesh, *Director General,* National Council of Applied Economic Research, **India**

Morand, Pascal, *Executive Director,* Institut Français de la Mode, **France**

Mphahlele, Es'kia, *Education Consultant, Author, and Professor of Literature,* University of Witwatersrand, **South Africa**

Nickell, Stephen, *Professor and Director,* Institute of Economics and Statistics, University of Oxford, **UK**

Rosen, David, *Chief Rabbi; Director,* Anti-Defamation League, Israel Office; *International President,* World Conference on|Religion and Peace, **Israel**

Schwab, Klaus, *Founder and President,* World Economic Forum, **Switzerland**

Searle, John R., *Professor, Philosophy of Mind and Language,* University of

California, Berkeley, **USA**

Shimada, Haruo, *Professor of Economics,* Keio University, **Japan**

Spivakov, Vladimir, *Violinist, Conductor, and President,* Vladimir Spivakov
International Charity Foundation, **Russia**

Tutu, Desmond M., *Archbishop Emeritus and Chairperson,* Truth and Recon-
ciliation Commission, **South Africa**

Walter, Ingo, *Professor of Applied Financial Economics and Director,* Salomon
Center, New York University, **USA**

Wiesel, Elie, *Professor of the Humanities,* Boston University, **USA**

Diplomats

Al-Thani, Fahad Awaida, *Ambassador and Permanent Representative of Qatar
to the United Nations, Geneva,* **Qatar**

Annan, Kofi, *Secretary-General of the United Nations,* **UN**

Arlacchi, Pino, *Undersecretary General of the United Nations and Executive
Director of the Office for Drug Control and Crime Prevention, Venice,* **Italy**

Bekic, Drako, *Ambassador and Permanent Representative of the Republic of
Croatia to the United Nations, Geneva,* **Croatia**

Castillero, Juan A., *Extraordinary Ambassador of Panama to Switzerland,*
Panama

Gadaud, André, *Ambassador of France to Switzerland,* **France**

Gomes, Goncalo de Santa Clara, *Ambassador and Permanent Representative of
Portugal to the United Nations, Geneva,* **Portugal**

Harbinson, Stuart, *Permanent Representative of Hong Kong to the World Trade
Organization, Geneva,* **Hong Kong**

Jokonya, Tichaona J.B., *Ambassador and Permanent Representative of
Zimbabwe to the United Nations, Geneva,* **Zimbabwe**

Balakrishnan, Kizhakke Pisharath, *Ambassador of India to Switzerland,*
India

Lamdan, Yosef, *Ambassador and Permanent Representative of Israel to the
United Nations, Geneva,* **Israel**

Loayza, Javier, *Chargé d'Affaires of Bolivia to the United Nations, Geneva,*
Bolivia

Maimeskoul, Mykola, *Ambassador and Permanent Representative of Ukraine to the United Nations, Geneva,* **Ukraine**

Matsunaga, Nobuo, *Special Envoy of the Government of Japan,* **Japan**

Padilla, Ezequiel, *Ambassador of Mexico to Switzerland,* **Mexico**

Pramudwinai, Don, *Ambassador Extraordinary and Plenipotentiary of Thailand to Switzerland,* **Thailand**

Ramlawi, Nabil, *Ambassador and Permanent Representative of the Palestinian Authority to the United Nations, Geneva,* **Palestine**

Richardson, Bill, *US Ambassador to the United Nations, New York,* **USA**

Wu Jianmin, *Ambassador and Permanent Representative of the People's Republic of China to the United Nations, Geneva,* **China**

Zahran, Mounir, *Ambassador and Permanent Representative of Egypt to the United Nations, Geneva,* **Egypt**

Scientists, Mystics, Technoprophets

Berners-Lee, Tim, *Director,* World Wide Web Consortium; *Principal Research Scientist,* Massachusetts Institute of Technology Laboratory for Computer Science, **USA**

Chaum, David, *Founder and Chief Technology Officer,* Digicash BV, **Netherlands**

Cohen, Daniel, *Chief Genomics Officer,* Genomics Research Center, GEN-SET, **France**

Crutzen, Paul J., *Director,* Atmospheric Chemistry Division, Max-Planck Institute for Technology, **Germany**

Dertouzos, Michael L., *Director,* MIT Laboratory for Computer Science and *Professor of Computer Science and Electrical Engineering,* Massachusetts Institute of Technology, **USA**

Huber, Martin C. E., *Head,* Space Science Department, ESTEC/ESA, **Netherlands**

de Kerckhove, Derrick, *Director,* The McLuhan Program in Culture and Technology, Univeristy of Toronto, **Canada**

Lanier, Jaron, *Visiting Scholar,* Columbia University; *Lead Scientist,* National Tele-Immersion Initiative, **USA**

Marks, Joan H., *Director of the Human Genetics Program,* Sarah Lawrence College, **USA**

McGowan, Alan H., *Director, Public Understanding of Science,* American Association for the Advancement of Science (AAAS), **USA**

Negroponte, Nicholas, *Director,* Media Laboratory; *Professor of Media Technology,* Massachusetts Institute of Technology; *Chairman,* 2B1 Foundation, **USA**

Peccoud, Dominic, *Jesuit Priest; Member,* French National Academy of Engineering (CADAS), **France**

de Rosnay, Joël, *Director of Strategy,* Cité des Science et de l'Industrie, **France**

Saffo, Paul, *Director,* Institute for the Future, **USA**

Schapowal, Andreas G., *Senior Lecturer and Head,* Unit of Allergology and Environmental Medicine, Hannover Medical School, **Germany**

Sunyaev, Rashid A., *Director,* Max-Planck Institute for Astrophysics, Germany; *Head,* High Energy Astrophysics Department, Space Research Institute, Russian Academy of Sciences, Moscow, **Russia**

Tapscott, Donald, *Chairman,* Alliance for Converging Technologies, **Canada**

Warwick, Kevin, *Professor of Cybernetics,* University of Reading, **UK**

Woo, Chia-Wei, *President,* Hong Kong University of Science and Technology, **Hong Kong**

Zinkernagel, Rolf M., *Director,* Institute of Experimental Immunology, University of Zurich, **Switzerland**